An Interesting Detail

An Interesting Detail

KIMBERLY CAMPANELLO

BLOOMSBURY POETRY

LONDON · OXFORD · NEW YORK · NEW DELHI · SYDNEY

BLOOMSBURY POETRY

Bloomsbury Publishing Plc

50 Bedford Square, London, WC1B 3DP, UK

29 Earlsfort Terrace, Dublin 2, Ireland

BLOOMSBURY, BLOOMSBURY POETRY and the Diana logo
are trademarks of Bloomsbury Publishing Plc

First published in Great Britain, 2025

Grateful acknowledgement to Édouard Louis for permission to reprint
the line ‹des corps fatigués des mains fatiguées des dos broyés des regards
épuisés› (@edouard_louis via X, 04.12.2018: https://x.com/edouard_louis/
status/1069956833287245824)

A catalogue record for this book is available from the British Library

ISBN: PB: 978-1-5266-8059-4;
eBook: 978-1-5266-9061-6; ePDF: 978-1-5266-9062-3

2 4 6 8 10 9 7 5 3 1

Typeset by Laura Jones-Rivera
Printed and bound in Great Britain by
Clays Ltd, Elcograf S.p.A.

To find out more about our authors and books
visit www.bloomsbury.com and sign up for our newsletters
For product safety related questions contact productsafety@bloomsbury.com

A door slammed and in the village square
the child spun his arms around, along with
the weather vanes and cocks up on towers
of every place, beneath the dazzling rain.

– Arthur Rimbaud, 'After the Flood' from *Illuminations*

Contents

I'd love to be able to say I've been there

to gaze out over the water
in the correct location
and hear its bells ringing
you can hear the bells of the church ring
you can hear the muffled sounds
of the city's bells tolling
far beneath the waves
if you want to hear the bells
beneath the waves
try the left side of the beach
this opening sequence sounds
incredibly akin
to the ringing of cathedral bells echoing
from beneath the sea
it's almost as if we can hear the gentle
tolling of church bells
from well beneath
the surface of the sea
folklore asserts that the bells
of the churches can still be heard
below the waters
of the bay
church bells can still be heard
ringing there
below the waters of the bay
locals say that on a quiet day
the bells of the city can be heard
below the waves

when the weather
is very quiet one may hear the bells
ring from the disappeared city
when the sea is calm one can hear
the bells of the church ringing
from the depths of the bay
it is said
that on stormy nights
you can hear the sound of the ghostly
bells ringing out across the waters
the rise of a cathedral
from the water
and subsequent return to the depths complete
with bells chiming, priests chanting, organ playing
when it is calm we can just make out
amid the echoes and the afterthoughts, the quiet
ringing of the bells
from beneath the sea,
a haunting, mesmerizing sound
the drowned city, in the bay,
is said to have church bells which still
ring when the sea is rough
only the cathedral, symbol of the decent
and devout people, enjoys any kind
of afterlife, as it is said to rise up
out of the watery depths on clear days
at sunrise, the ringing bells and booming organ
audible across the expanse of the bay,
before sinking back into the sea by night
it's still said that when the tide is low,
the towers of the city can be seen
just below the surface,

sometimes the bells
from the cathedral can still be heard
ringing from the depths of the sea
on the day it happens,
the first person who sees the church's spire
or hears the sound
of its bells will become king
of the city and all its territory
and then I read a little more
about the city and the bells
of the cathedral
ringing underwater on a still day

THE TREE

We drove out from our village and into the stars. We wanted a fire to stare into. The trees were otherly, unplanted by human hands, and so we tied them up with our favourite things. The neighbouring island had a tree for meetings that resembled democracy. It was eventually worn to pieces and so the people carried bits away and shellacked them for their mantlepieces. Around the fire in the field there were speculations about the nature of reality and stories I am certain could not be true. Could every random strip of land have once been a battlefield and a site of plague, famine and holy significance? You said if we wait long enough in one spot the cycle will start again. I said the sound system is just about equal to this sort of thing.

An Interesting Detail

An interesting detail in the history of this church involves 813 martyrs' skulls embedded in the chapel wall. The glass covering was added in the mid-twentieth century to shield the skulls from dust and thereby save on labour costs. I have written about this before, but you may or may not have noticed it in my files. It pertains to the cheekbones of the martyrs and the significance of their height and prominence. The cheekbones are reaching for the stars, one might say, and consistently so. The prominence of the mind or the head in the abiding orientation of Western thought may have something to do with the fact that it takes so long for the skull to decay, particularly in dry climates where over the years so much civilisation has plunged its crusted root into the earth again and again. Imagine how different everything would be if the womb was visible to us in the first place and if it could resist the rot and hold its shape for hundreds or even thousands of years. Notably, in one of the three forests mentioned in the tale you will find a café selling paninis in paper wrappers and water in plastic bottles. The child blows his whistle, continuously, and no one will try and stop him. This probably relates to the rampant drug use in the city in recent times and the way in which one is encouraged to accept it and walk on by. I, for one, noticed her cheekbones slicing cold air from beneath hood and hair.

THE GYM

You obtain a free gym off the internet for the back garden. This makes it easier to isolate muscles individually or in groups in full view of the neighbours whose windows look out over our slack bodies moving objects unnecessarily. In actual fact the earliest humans probably did have similar hand weights or focused exercise technologies, though the common argument still stands that as some moved away from needing to do physical work to survive, we lost our suppleness and so our health. Our life spans are indeed extended, but this is due to medical interventions which have nothing to do with me and my own efforts beyond potential agreement in their value and support through taxation. And those bumpy stone objects found in the furthest reaches of the northern islands. Were they shot puts or hand weights created to prepare the muscles for necessary hunting and grappling. Were they invented to prime the experience of the actual. Unfortunately, they show no evidence of being thrown and likely spent their days in pristine ritual condition swaddled in skins associated with high status that have now disintegrated, though it is possible that the only ones to have been collected and so thought typical are the most ornamental, the least damaged.

THE TOWER

This is the order. The tower remembered the war. At the tower our language was different. There was a revolution and the tower remembered it. We held hands in the woods near the tower. The tower was the backdrop for fireworks. At the tower I remembered my father was allergic to bee stings. Kids drank beer by the fence around the tower. We never touched the tower though at a distance our feet filled old prints. We went around the tower to avoid abandoned ordnance. On my birthday we went to the tower. The mansion by the tower was burned by criminals. The tower remembered virginity was a concept. We went to the tower but could not reach it. The tower was hollow and its passages were stone. The tower wondered what language the men were speaking. The city developed plans to make the tower accessible to the public. The tower was taken in open revolt. The tower witnessed ecstatic touch. The invaders planted bombs in the tower during the war. At the tower I remembered a bee flew into a hole in my jeans and stung my thigh. We stripped each other naked in the trees by the tower. The tower saw the bay. There was a revolution and the tower remembered it. A private estate located itself around you, the tower, the order of memory.

THE LANGUAGE

The books don't know what's inside their covers, or they don't care. Just when you learned what was happening, what direction to face, how to move and what to carry where, the language changed. You were reassured it was all still working and the transformation would be total, just as before. We could just as easily go to the top of the dune and play with roots in the sand. We could even kneel down and twist them around our hands and wrists to hold ourselves down. As I understand it, the heart can be seen to beat if you can get a glow to show up properly around it. Any background will do.

Exam

I was making do with the costumes and repetitions available to me in a new place. The previous night you carried up bundles of perfumes, incense, fabrics and jewellery to store in my room. Our meal was a canned vegetable dish from a petrol station shelf. It steamed my windows and we fell easefully to the floor. In time a fallow scent wrecked the merchandise. Though we suitably oiled ourselves for all activities we still caused each other pain. I took exams that required me and hundreds of others to consider such cases from various angles and in a range of contexts. Each time I filled the lined notebook, every page. Each time I handed in early and left.

THE OLD PLATTER

We brought out one of my grandmother's old platters at dinner last night. The green ceramic platter used on Sundays. We all know her story so I don't need to elaborate here. I was instantly reminded of my nomadic clinging to places and people and the way that dishes are sadly the last thing you'd think of bringing along on a major move these days even though they did once feature in ship burials due to their symbolic and familial significance. The burials and hoards you find dotted around show this phenomenon very well. There's money and armour, of course, and jewellery, but also textiles and shoes, very well preserved. On top of all that is a huge platter with stamps that show it was a century old when buried and had been made in the capital of a distant empire.

SIMPLE TUNIC

I always wear the same simple tunic. I always pair it with the same PVC leggings. The tunic and the leggings slip through my letterbox and I slip them on. They always fit. I am shown the tunic and leggings all day and all night. That's me there, I think. That's me without a head wearing the tunic. My skin tone shifts. My hands on my hips de-age. No more baggy knuckles. On the other hand, near the castle they have found skeletons. Isotopic testing of the teeth shows a diversity of genetic origins and time spent abroad eating in Spain, North Africa, and so on. The milk teeth from the children show this best. The sea washed away the shore and these so-called bowl hole burials were held up as examples – bodies placed face down, bodies curled up on their sides, bodies supine on their backs. The meaning of these varied customs is a matter for debate. In a similar manner, it's in doubt whether hair that accumulates in your drain should be put in the toilet and flushed away or tossed in the bin. Contact lenses should not be flushed. That much is clear.

You were at your gate

The tomatoes you had grown were drying in a small wagon. Your wedding all those years ago had been an intimate affair. The photograph sent across the ocean came back to you in my hand. A similar understanding of kinship is found among bricks or stone used in church buildings or fortresses. They return in a new form by way of a country manor house, a stable, or a shrine holding beer bottles. I have returned recently from sabbatical. The working conditions there are appalling. A line-up of knots needed four bodybuilders to massage out of me. They fingered my sinews and released my fascia. My pectoral muscles, for example, were utterly botched. The myth of the whiteness of classicism is equally gripping. Something about it is suggestive of the power washer. There was one of them used a few years ago on a local guildhall. They lost all the wood carvings trying to get at the stone.

THE WELL

The well had been full of trash, which the archaeologists appreciated. Now bars criss-cross the lip to prevent us from gathering its waters. The tipis where they serve gin are always busy. The daffodils have a symbolic number of petals to mark the massacre. I could murder a steak burger or a stew. You will have noticed that I've made every effort to explain to visitors which wall is from which century and how it seems only one book survived that particular transition. This piped-in smell of the past has me starving.

MEASURING DISTANCES

The fish in the case were looking shocked to find themselves laid over chipped ice. Though of course they couldn't feel a thing. The bread was suitably crusty and dredged a channel, as desired, through my cold soup. This is how the opening of the review went, but I didn't buy it. Instead, I referred you to three inches of candle wax covering the pavements between the two churches on opposite sides of the city, as well as the minute measurements required to build the passage tombs located in several other not-too-far-away places we have been. I underscored my point by drawing you the icon throwing light from one hand to the other, if that is indeed what is happening. The figure so depicted, and depicted so often, is measuring distances. I tell you this is why we come here to get away from it all.

MOVING NOWHERE HERE

A rosy sanctuary will I dress
With the wreath'd trellis of a working brain
— John Keats, 'Ode to Psyche'

begins with shouting
in sleep I am naked
on the carpet in a power stance
sensing an army nearby
I am charging the ghost
hanging on the back of the door
I am trapped inside the Shimmer
boxed into fetal position
in a spice cupboard
between jars filled with dried Leaves

⁓

it continues in waking life
with food and drink
brought on trays
for what seems like no reason
I must be propped on pillows
to attempt anything at all
other than dream

⁓

it continues with rarely
sometimes or often
feeling achingly ancient

~

I continue to await
the perspective this feeling
ought to bring

~

but I refuse
teleological notions of progress
especially when what is meant
by progression is me Moving
slowly or quickly
into a state in which I cannot
Move or Move with ease
anywhere and everywhere
on my own

~

that sounds to me
like regression
or like Moving down
a very screwy road
on an old map

~

I am on my own
and I am not
having an emotional jag
in which I remember

Something isn't circulating
or being produced properly
Something that Flows
in what I used to (still) think
is the very site of me
you see this Something
will not issue forth will not Flow

⁓

I am avoiding technical
language in the hope there might
be some double (multiple?) meanings
to be felt Here in the basics

⁓

meaning the Something
that Flows (or in this case
doesn't Flow) in the very
site of me (you)

⁓

technical language would allow you (me)
to say not me (you) though you (I)
could say not me (you) yet

⁓

I am afraid to say we are all
progressing or regressing

down a more or less screwy road
found on a very old map
until
we are going Nowhere

∽

I promise you he says
I am going Nowhere
regardless
of this

∽

I may not
be able to
swallow this
or anything
one day
because of it

∽

not jagging on my own
I am stacking some pages
I just printed I am slamming
the stack's edge against the table
to see how thick
my book is becoming

~

it is not thick enough
without this poem
to bear the weight
of this poem

~

I see that my Hand
is barely trembling
Something is Flowing

~

and in my book the I's
are confused throughout
about what they know about it all
and by it all I mean it all
not simply the subject
of this poem which I fear
is all you will forevermore
read in the language
I put down for you

~

I am putting this subject down
Here in language now
for one time and one time only
when this poem ends it ends god
dammit but of course I know that's not
how these things work

~

I know what I am getting into
and what you're getting out of it
and when this poem ends
I am Here shaking still

~

I am shopping for a wedding dress
and one dress is called the X dress
it is named for the Something
that will not Flow Here
at the very site of me

~

do you have difficulty
dressing yourself

~

often sometimes never

~

I want to at least have good nails
I want to shake
like a Leaf wearing green polish
on alternate nails and hot pink on the rest

〜

in general with this
to live my best life
I have to be the boulder
that the river Flows around

〜

is that a cliché
or something my counsellor
or trade union told me to say
am I a boulder or the boulder
can I be the boulder
if there are other boulders
and who or what is the river

〜

here is the river
I walk beside every day
(I walk beside it now
every day while I still can)

〜

I am not a boulder
when I walk
beside this river
often I have wished
we could hold each other's
trembling Hands and Move together

~

feelings get stirred up
based on conditions
that I must identify and optimise
for instance my foot in a shoe
against the ground
I must find the exact amount
of feedback to my foot
from shoe top and shoe bottom
in relation to the type of surface
to remind my feet
that we are Here on earth
for now and it's perfectly ok
to keep on Moving

~

you are young she says
you must train it
while you can
and hope to retain it

~

the way forward
is to make the hardest things
even harder and do all this
while speaking a foreign language
or subtracting down by nines or sevens
from a high odd number

~

he continues to be impressed
by the way
I have thrown myself
into activity

~

I am threatened physically
by a jerk honking his horn
and when I snap back
and insist on respect
I find I am shaking maximally
shakes like I have never
seen surface on myself or others
not even in war footage or
that ecstatic dance class

~

the onlooker says
you are ok you can
calm down now
I say I am very calm
and I am not ok

~

I can see why you'd be upset
by that reaction he says
people don't like to think

23

about death and your Movement
problems Move their thoughts toward death
and suddenly you are like the Dark Mother
who nurtures and brings dissolution

⌣

note that this is not a full
account of my experience
and bear in mind experiences
differ from person to person

⌣

not everyone suffers everything
it is possible to suffer
in time or ever

⌣

could you write Something for me
he says and then he says
you may have difficulty writing

⌣

my writing is illegible and the words
have become so very small so
very crowded on the page

~

my writing is building up a picture
of what is wrong with me

~

I search for poets
definitely Diane di Prima
maybe Samuel Beckett
(definitely his mother)

~

the next time I see him
my written Something
is in his folder
it says I can write like this

~

he turns the page
to the Shimmering spiral
I had concentrated
hard and drawn

~

each new person is always asking
about the origin story
of the destruction that is happening
at the very site of me

~

there is a technical language
that explains all this

~

I will not use it

~

instead I will say that today
with my Flowing river
I crossed the edge
of a thunderstorm
I Moved
from pelting rain into
Shimmering sun
and it was like
it always has been on the edge
of storms I have seen
and storms I know only in poems

~

concentrated and hard
with Something Moving
often Nowhere
Here like a Leaf Flowing
around a boulder
carried by trembling Hands of water

Forms

First, you must fill this one out, making sure you do not exceed the edge. Afterwards, a plot will be offered to you and then further forms after that. If you take up the plot, you must follow through. I was in your position at one time, straddling water and stone, looking down but not seeing far, in the character of a knight with an axe wound. I reversed and it all fell through. If you circle the edge, you are around but not beyond it and this makes things feel melancholy as if accompanied by a lute. So I really can't say much more about it other than to use the guidance as best you can.

SIMPLE ECO POEM

I used to check rudimentary online mail that came from New York City from the profile name BleekrPoet who was actually Gustave Charpentier's great-grandson. We sent each other poems and pictures of Morrissey. Now anything and everything to do with Morrissey belongs in the landfill along with the plastic cups that Harry and Sally drank from. Harry and Sally had bumped into each other at the airport and ended up talking on the plane. It was pre-recycling and post-handcrafted. John Dewey warned us. The sun is a burnished orb like our popcorn popper that plugged into the wall on Hunters Ct. One time it started smoking. Weed killer is called Round-up. The people at the borders are always somewhere nearby. The plastic cups in the scene from the film are eternity. It takes far far longer and many many more arguments to refurb the visitor's centre at the passage tomb than to build the passage tomb itself. The sun is a burnished orb except now we are less responsive to it, even at equinox. We hold our talismans and our scribbled notes and burn plants with no cultural significance, for us. It turns out popcorn interferes with or leads to the development of polyps. It's no surprise that at Thanksgiving we wish we had never happened upon the world.

THE SNAKE

The snake gave me a fix. I hadn't known the cost. All the while I bought bread, I bought cherries. I made simple meals and the snake said no worries. I did four or five new dishes a week. I ran them by the snake and he said sure. I swallowed them all. He swallowed them all. We grew different. In the old stables lives a lady who sometimes lends me butter. She says it has to stop. These horseshoes above the doorframes don't seem to be doing their job. I am drowning in plastic bags. I have nothing to hold. Everything I make passes through us. The back wall is crumbling and one day it will fall.

Circulation

Bodies circle the park at a good clip. An increasingly regular activity. A spin or ramble through a city denuded of visitors. I try to settle in. We've been circulating too much, like substances, like blood in the body. Some writers become irritated when blood is depicted as red. They believe blue to be its actual colour as shown by ancient hierarchies and modern-day charts. The underground tombs are open now, the ones created when the graveyards were denuded of their occupants. In the northern islands they have found abandoned cities with beds dug into the earth, including some extant stone pillows. We should imagine people had some kind of bedding to make it more comfortable before they fled.

Receipt

One remarkable item, found with a man buried near where I used to live, turned out to be a whistle made from a carved and highly polished human thigh bone. Dating suggests it belonged to someone who lived around the same time as him. To bring you up to speed on this, I'm certain they could squeeze me in here among the greats. It's what I want. It's important to let people know your wishes in advance. Especially kids who have never made pilgrimages like this one even though they live nearby and express an interest in surpassing rudimentary notions of suffering and reason. The shells at the base of certain walls can either be seen as detritus or decoration, reminiscent of a cake that shoots memory through your body and is itself reminiscent of a body we feel it is important to keep nearby, but not to approach at all times, just as we manage saints, disarticulating and placing them in boxes and dotting them around the world awaiting special exposure, or a duck that has been cooked a certain way to allow it to collapse in on itself until we are ready to release it from its can for eating. I feel like I really miss her and I never even met her in person. The simplicity of her initials carved there is really strong for me. I've thought a lot about it and I appreciate you taking this information forward to spread among interested parties. I'm just going to slide my pencil here in this pot and hope for the best. You might want to place a stone or a slip of paper, like a receipt.

THE TABLE

In a minor but unrelenting way I made sure I could still eat it. I was happy to look it in the eye when it was brought out. I lifted the lashed lid. The others at the table were more or less content. Its eyes were blue and her eyes were blue. I believed she was from somewhere else simply because of her vowels. Wanting and wishing and vowing and sermon are all the same and were the same in her mouth. But there was something else. Possibly the word for the dish. When she offered it, it slid toward omen. The brain was good-sized, well flavoured with itself. I thought about its thoughts. I wondered what it wondered. For the briefest of moments I saw sky and smelled grass and shit. I stayed quiet. I left the others to their devices. When it was time to pay I brought down my briefcase from the brass rack overhead. I handed out the brochures. I explained the specificity of the offer. I explained the driving force. I made sure they understood. Consider me a visionary, I argued. I have never seen the inside of my oesophagus though one man actually has. Proprioception is a timely topic, one of them offered. A snake swallowing its tail.

New Seeds

We were trying to rid ourselves of the trees. We cut into them, poisoned their wounds, fired their crowns. They released new seeds and spread. We opened up to each other about it. These trees were brought here. Some of us were brought here or we were released and we spread. She fried me some bread in her pan to go with the dangerous animal I was eating. A road cuts across, she said, just take it to the edge and keep going.

The Permissions

In the interpretive centre I stepped into the priest-hole first. On the track I heard whispers and the unsheathing of swords. I'm fine, I said. Her glowing dot travelled twice over the Alps and back, on foot, to ask men for permissions. The relic kept behind the curtain in a jar is a tiny hand of another woman I really like. Back then the priest's vestments had to be hidden under a display of cloth and notions. That evening we ate fast and practised the compound past tense. Pasta is described as ribbons, sometimes as flesh hanging from a frame. Or when dried it's the name of a woman with reference to her deadly hair.

GRAVEL

I have mentioned gravel to you before. The fact that the river has gone so high, unprecedentedly high, and hidden all the banks and their paths, all the places where nature's stones live and are thrown. So our gravel chips, mined and crushed and shovelled into key places and blown back out of them, are all I have on hand to meditate upon, to help me think this through. How can it be that the waters are so close and their contents so out of reach? There are graves down there. Bodies and objects made by ancient hands make this town an attractive destination. People sleep in tents along those banks. And not for fun. On the sidewalk today, an apple core, a dark stone and a small dog, chained. I picked one up.

Major Insights

She's taken to hanging what I send above her chair, most recently the chart depicting the ancient king found buried with his dog, four horses, cattle and sheep. Major insights will be garnered as a result. I told her right away about the man spray-painting the yard to mark the line. No need to feel intimidated without explanation. She said she didn't want me to see under her sink. I said it's not clean down there in anyone's house. I had brought lunch. I said I was hunting paper towel.

An Indicator

Shaving and oiling the insides of a horse's ears is beneficial for those who will support it. The electric shave reveals past histories. Bites under scabs. Then you can rub the oil into the fold with the side of your hand, sliding it and turning it to bring your thumb to the base where the unique nub pulses near the skull. I wrote a unique letter outlining the basics. The shape of the fish and its correspondence to my own body. The cup, too. I described the urges of the universe and the least and most likely outcomes of penance and celebration. Electric air is an indicator of the storm on the horizon. The horizon, you write back, yours or mine?

THE SUN LOUNGER

In order to rest and take the sun I ordered a sun lounger the colour of the sun. It arrived and proved useful. In the sun lounger I attempted to read important passages about clashes between our ancestors. The key statements about killing and ravishing (which is rape) are found in the text. Even though I desired the sun I did try to remain clothed in my back garden out of consideration for the neighbours. I pulled my trouser legs up as far as they would go but elastic around the calves cut off circulation to my thighs. It was not a perfect system. The weather let me down and I spent most of the time inside, unfolding the lounger for only a few short and pleasant intervals. The confusion about the DNA we carry is persistent. Similarly, in contrast to our ancestors' vivid depictions of creatures, their abstractions – simple scratchings and apparently aimless lines – throw up few coherent interpretations. When not lounging I painted the walls white and red.

THE FREEZER

I should also mention that I have meat shame. If you examine the trays you can probably tell which ones are for meat (no air holes for sealing) and which ones are for fruit and veg (air holes for breathing). I have emptied one of the big meat trays of its meat, separated pieces into various plastic bags and put them in the freezer to stop time. It stops (actually, it slows) time. That's why from time to time and more so especially now, tourists and climbers come across ancient time-stopped bodies in the colder regions. They are well preserved and we can examine what they wore – such as their shoes which are quite complex and indicative of the existence of a cobbler profession. We can remove their stomachs and intestines to see and smell their last meals. Like ibex meat. Or chamois meat. And red deer meat. And herb bread.

Ghost Walk

All those years walking great distances across capital cities during strikes. My body sliding off me like melted butter. A ghost self walking to the worst jobs I ever had. You always said that if you saw a ghost walking everything about your life would have to change. Lines of theories and experimentation torn apart by a column of soldiers marching through the cellar at the level of your knees. In my current state I report I can walk to the corner shop but there is pain and humiliation. In reply I get more detail is needed. What is particularly hilarious is that I envy commuters on foot taking vital steps. It's all in the journey. Miles on your body clock. Covering a great distance gives you wisdom. Otherwise kind people say things like my body or my brain is on strike. A fragment of underdone potato or the medications we take to move and to think. Haven't we all seen, haven't we all touched the wounds in the flesh and in the mind with the tips of our fingers or the edges of our eyes. Pain like laying the sole of one foot over the top of the other and driving a nail through. I often sit on the wall part way and cry. More detail. At first, the river is a squiggle in the canyon bottom, a simple sign you can't fathom. You walk so far down, so deep, you can't establish the sign's relationship to the canyon, to what the squiggle has made. Evidence attached. Is it our evolved capacity to feel and so insist that we are not alone, never have been and that our limbs work in concert with those of the past. Imperative to take up your mat. Rate the pain. Detail. There was also a horse stepping through the cellar dragging a cart, disappearing into the wall. The child who haunts this place could not walk. The lights go on and off. The guide prompts us to scream. The horse and then the cart and then the tree and then before. More. We aren't supposed to use the heart and board to make contact. Test walk. Timed. Would you normally rest by now. For how long.

GROWTH

I might have told you this before, but we used to catch and re-lease them in our darkened house and let them glow. Now their light is hardly detectable. If you coil yourself forward tightly enough you can see into your own entry and exit points and locate the sand that got in through the legs of your suit. You can watch it trying to enter you and also appreciate yourself trying to pull it in. There are periods of growth you can't sense but can see happen, some lights on, some lights out.

USE VALUE

If I had studied
STEM things might
have been different.
If I had fed
into the meeting
there would have
been an outcome.
The tin whistle
is a passion of mine.
Aren't I lucky
to do what I'm
passionate about?
Someone back in the day
was breastfeeding
foundlings. The clash
of bodies resembling
certain kinds of sex.
I am as useful
to society as this
drenched napkin
on the pavement
held together and down
by its former shape.
When the sun comes out
at last my flecks will
go flying. The grips have
come off the handles
but steering is still possible.
Who are you? Where are you?
Is that what you said?

unpadded kneelers and a framed poem on the shrine wall for
saint margaret clitherow pressed
to death on lady day good
friday her zeal led her to harbour
spread out on the ground sharp
stone at her back pray for us

amenorrhoea

Did she have children? Or was faith her focus?

oh england thy fruit in the fields in the trees rotting thy work
and pensions pressed on bor-
rowed time wrong word stollen
sugar and butter this year foreign
merry christmas surge in spend-
ing drone takedown pray for us

amenorrhoea

Yes, but did she have her own children?

des corps fatigués des mains fatiguées des dos broyés des regards
épuisés (édouard louis) pathetic
even tragic commentary on life
as it is ordinarily lived (john

dewey) pressed you will get
two breaks the cage will open
automatically step out pray for us

amenorrhoea

So are you going to have kids or what?

sedimentary suffering which ground where doesn't matter
arms wide open hands open for
rain in the grave not like jesus
risen up there's got to be some
other hands down there to touch
tiny morsels of flesh and bone
left underground an archaeolog-
ical dig cordoned off pray for us

amenorrhoea

Evidence of prior pregnancy?

writing religion they will come for me she was seen in chapels
with relics eyeing clitherow's hand
in a bell jar she was seen in sacré
coeur that dreadful basilica atone-
ment for la commune there are
good guys and bad guys and she
was definitely sitting there next
to a trump voter she was weeping

at the sight of people weeping at
the sight of the sacrament which
war are we fighting now any-
way which bot the usage at the
time 1586 atonement no doubt

amenorrhoea

Does she have children? Does she confess it in writing?

the bodies seen bodies who has seen bodies weep at the sight of
them being seen had the baby
turned before the door a heavy
blanket was brought down
upon her unbearably weighted

amenorrhoea

Will you have children?

BETTER VIEW

lord's convenience
village stage left
crows hillocks
snaking smoke foil
gorge railway plot
oldest human habitation
site dead rats test
omphalos atmosphere
palimpsest apotropaic
hail marys diamonds
horse head utmost
importance bird song
understood travel lodge
repeat power unsung night
bore hole geology won't
support flicker blast yearn

They didn't expect

hedges steeples the time it takes
to cut away the chutes purpling
lips down the promenade past
nations stepping forward fire
blocking fire important speech
looped in a darkened room
hardy sightseers in rainproof
jackets everlasting bunkers
farmers or farmers wives or
farmers children blown
up mundane tasks running
commentary along the bottom
of the tapestry build up
of bodies where do we go
when we die the lovers
eating their crêpes her
outrageously classy flowers
their rolling cigarettes like sex

FAMILY WALK

The family walk the sandbar for sand dollars, slip them between toes, foot to hand, and bucket them. The dollars dry to death on the condo patio. The family walk to the cave paintings. They find a wild horse in a sinkhole just before it dries to death at the level of their knees. The family leave the horse, certain that helicopters will come and drop in a tree. The family walk on soil made of tiny creatures that hold together the desert. The family walk the glacier. They place their feet on nails driven into the ice, hold onto ropes circling the face. Before you know it, the glacier lets go of the nails and shrugs the ropes. The family walk the park, cover great distances into the past and into fantasy, swallow sour chipped ice, wait for an explosive ride. The line folds thousands of walkers into itself. All the second skin on shredded feet. The family walk the spine of the island and stop. Boots off in the lake they take on leeches, tear them off. The patriarch's bloody walk in bad shoes in the last century.

FAULT

A call was made to a team of specialist coroners who would work with local volunteers. The team arrived and the layers were cut back. When they reached the flesh everyone said 'I'm feeling so hungry' at the exact same time. Later the son held her eyeball in his arms. That is the photo I received. Afternoon passed and organs came out. It was clear this time that the fault was not with us. Instead, the cause of death had arisen from organisms living in the fish she had eaten. They had infiltrated her system and shredded her heart. The team was somewhat relieved. She was twice as long as my house is deep. The day is remembered as a good experience.

SAGE

In her cottage on the edge we kept everything on. The glasses and plates wore previous tastes. The cat guarded the carcass on the floor and a photo of a son was taped to the wall above the fire. The sea worked away beneath us, making haste to bring us closer. In the morning I couldn't find my hat though I had slept wearing it. Years later in one of the significant forests a sign explained the disappearance of the mythical lake. The lack of undergrowth meant there were few insects and therefore birds. Laughter shook the deer from their poses. If this is wisdom, it is lost on me.

A Few Words

I've been asked to sum up in a few words how we measure space, which of course relates to how we measure time. The point of departure ought to be the black plastic cover laid at the foot of the gutter's descending pipe. It blocks out leaves, animals and mud from entering the water return and therefore the sewer system, but the cover is not nailed down and so it has blown away across the yard and further down toward the back gate and the bomb shelter. I'm not certain why the birds don't feed on the seed we've put out for them or why the only sounds I can hear are of construction vehicles and buses indicating their reversal rather than children playing or rain falling. The school and the depot are equidistant from the table situated inside my house behind the newly installed door with its keys still in the lock. It is rainy out there. I thought I could make a fairly good soup without blending it, but it turns out its constituent parts don't work well together when apprehended on their own terms.

Packaging

I am thinking now of your packaging. What you've kept aside to show me and how much of it there is. The languages that cover each piece. The diagrams and bar codes. The semiotics of branding echoing with the spiral or the zigzag carvings found at sites across continents and periods. The way things can hold other things, and once inside, things are able to change from one state to another. The holy mother who saved us from plague and the insistence we dedicate two festive weeks per year to her. The thawing mountainside. The green bottle found the other day with the body that was born in 1947 missing since the 1980s. My bottles are lined up along the floor of my kitchen. Will I put them in my suitcase with my other packaging and bring them to you? If the plane crashes or the disease reaches my destination before me what will these things mean?

MAKE UP

From what I recall, an old fall is what makes my hand shake, which brings about its own particular limitations and flourishes. As a result, it can be easier to emphasise the symbolic nature of any such activity in order to make up for those aspects that I am less adept at demonstrating, such as writing or slicing vegetables. If you wish I can pour you a glass of wine, but it is better if I make larger movements, like opening the corked bottle in one go. That is if I am to appear less vulnerable and more impressive, which I assume you prefer me to be.

THE RESPONSE

The abandoned yacht has sunk, or the water has risen, rolling down to the river from the invented landscape dreamed up in smoke and mud. It's understandable, you know, our quickness to judgement, our minute calibration of the possible, our settling for, our settling in, the rack we made to hold our knives and our resolve to sweat the onion slowly, to bring its layers together and let the flavours right down, sinking into sweet alchemy, down past heat, back to when our hands were wholly fused to each other, ready to spark, which was not all that long ago but also unfathomably past tense, so I'm not sure what conditional phrase to set up and how to get it running on my tongue and out from my mouth and still breathe in. The GIF in response depicts a long-haired child eating a bright onion, raw and whole, no text in the frame.

Ceremonial Landscape

Several socially and politically significant events have taken place here. Things to do with haircuts and headdresses and ritual partnering and sonic interventions, as well as unforeseen deaths. We put a single rose in the central chamber to mark the loss of one of our own to the way these things go much of the time. Curves, wet, speeds. Place-names changing. You can ask me for fuller detail on any of this, though it might be best to wait until the end. Graffiti only lasts so long due to the stone's composition and this climate. The view remains the same. Close your eyes and plug your ears and cast your mind back to a time prior to any possibility of your existence. Go ahead and open everything back up. Tune in as though you don't matter and nothing is being said or done for you. I promise I'll stay quiet.

The Open Tray of Hair Pins

To render them useful again meant picking them up and soaking them in an appropriate liquid, individually drying each one with a paper towel and replacing them in their variously sized compartments. This incident was followed by a discussion of driving infractions that arise as a result of satellites guiding you into inappropriate areas where it is captured on camera thereby generating a print-out of a ticket in a municipal office, page one of which is delivered to you by email, which entices you to seek it in its complete form in order to verify its authenticity. This is possible only with payment of a substantial fee. You were told by those more experienced in these matters to pay, no matter what, and to pay more than once, upon request. In contrast, a dinosaur called a bee hummingbird was found preserved in 99-million-year-old amber. Upon further examination we can see that the eye would have formed a cone, like the eye bones in owls. This indicates that the bee hummingbird had exceptional vision. Its well-preserved tongue could yield further insights. Animals that become very small have to deal with specific problems, like how to generate enough heat, or how to fit all your organs inside your body.

FRAMING A POSTER

I took the poster I bought on my recent travels to the framer and received an agreeable estimate for glass and wood to encase it. Then I picked up a few ingredients, fresh dill and canned beef consommé, at a nearby shop. Nostalgia for the trip surged up in me when I passed the cemetery where I had a chance encounter with the phrase Sacred to the Memory of used in this instance more amply than names on their own. Articles on the distribution of beads in burials and the extent to which husbandry transformed language flow have subsided in favour of an eternal return to the end of the world. The threads I have laid out here are harder to braid together into something durable. I seem to recall an old publication about the origins of language being found in music. How we are singing to make something clear, to make something strong.

THE FORT

For the roof we took a piece of burlap from the bottom of an old couch and overlaid it with pine boughs. We had read the books about the need for square holes to put our rifles through and the variety of plants that could be used in a stew. We were intent on making this work. There were squashes in the garden and we burst them open with rocks. We dug down and looked for ancient hammers and axes we were certain we would find, located as we were near a quarry and a riverbed. When it came to our beliefs we were flexible. We didn't ask each other what the situation would bring in this regard. I did find a feather, a worn stone and a torn page from a book arranged on a piece of bark in the corner where he slept. This made me think I should come up with something of my own and fast.

THE GIANTS

After the drowning of two wild swimmers, I left town in an increasingly tiny bus. At each roundabout the passengers felt closer. Men were shrinking and women getting larger. We would need to walk. Our strides lapped up country miles. Naked now, we gathered trees like flowers and laid our bouquets at the entrances of passage tombs. We loped along cairned paths dipping our tongues into placid waters. Otters swam into us and tweaked our bladders. Salmon laid eggs in our guts for the new season. The ice cream van crashed and was abandoned. Bogs dried out and ancient butter rotted. Memorials went to pieces and shoe leather blew away as it hit the air. We became giants to hold the world and we were good.

THE MONUMENT

The plan for the weekend is to go to the monument built over the blown-up monument across from the building that is now a monument down the road from the statues that are monuments and the garden that is a monument and the centres of learning and making that are monuments and the café with its scones and its tea served in leaky pots. The march will assemble there with relevant flowers and speeches. The parade, not unlike the coronation stone, is a roving monument that brings people out of doors and requires identification. I have built a small monument to you that is easily misunderstood. Its language moves toward ever simpler states. I have crossed out to declare and written to say. I have removed all names in favour of she and he and they. And I, precious you, is a monument, a style, that moves.

Acknowledgements

I am grateful to the editors of the following magazines for publishing earlier versions of these poems: *Abandoned Playground*, *Belfield Literary Review*, *Cambridge Literary Review*, *Granta*, *Junction Box*, *London Magazine*, *Poetry Ireland Review*, *Poetry Review* and *White Review*.

A video version of 'form ever follows function' was commissioned for the *gorse* / *The Pickled Body* exhibition in the Illuminations gallery at Maynooth University. The poem was included in the short pamphlet *running commentary along the bottom of the tapestry* (above / ground press) and in the anthology *Witches, Warriors, Workers: An Anthology of Contemporary Working Women's Poetry* (Culture Matters).

A video version of 'The Sun Lounger' appeared as part of the *Poem Atlas* online exhibition 'Escapisms'.

Some of these poems first emerged with support from a joint Markievicz Award for a collaboration with Dimitra Xidous and Annemarie Ní Churreáin from the Irish Arts Council / An Chomhairle Ealaíon and the Department of Culture, Heritage and the Gaeltacht. They were published in 2024 by The Salvage Press in *(S)worn State(s)*, in a limited letterpress edition.

A multimedia version of 'I'd love to be able...' was produced with support from the Irish Arts Council / An Chomhairle Ealaíon for *sorry that you were not moved*, created in collaboration with Christodoulos Makris and Fallow Media.

This collection was written with the support of residencies at the Heinrich Böll cottage on Achill Island and the Centre Culturel Irlandais in Paris.

I am especially grateful to my agent, Becky Thomas at Lewinsohn Literary, for her commitment to my work.

Special thanks to my editor, Kayo Chingonyi. His insightful and sensitive engagement with these poems, as a fellow poet I truly admire, spurred me on to continue writing through the vicissitudes of the pandemic, which coincided with my Parkinson's diagnosis.

Thanks also to Allegra Le Fanu and Elisabeth Denison, and the wonderful team at Bloomsbury.

I am grateful to the poets and digital/letterpress publishers with whom I have collaborated recently: Annemarie Ní Churreáin, Christodoulos Makris, Ian Maleny (Fallow Media), Jamie Murphy (The Salvage Press) and Dimitra Xidous. Thank you to Jon Hughes and archaeologists Mark Edmonds and Ben Elliott for letting me earwig during their collaborative project (*Soundtracks: Acoustic Horizons of Past and Present*).

Thank you to my friends, family, University of Leeds colleagues, and fellow poets and writers for giving me something good to eat or think about during the writing of this book. With special thanks to Fiona Becket, Gregory Campanello, Ailbhe Darcy, Anne-Marie Evans, Joanne Hayden, Sarah K. Perry and Tiffany A. Tondut – who also did the cover painting.

Jon Hughes makes writing and life possible and fun.

A Note on the Author

Kimberly Campanello's recent poetry publications include *MOTHERBABYHOME* (zimZalla, 2019), *sorry that you were not moved* (Fallow Media, 2022) and *(S)worn State(s)* (The Salvage Press, 2024). Her debut novel, *Use the Words You Have*, is forthcoming from Somesuch Editions in 2025. She is Professor of Poetry at the University of Leeds.

A Note on the Type

Warnock is a serif typeface designed by Robert Slimbach. The design features sharp, wedge-shaped serifs. The typeface is named after John Warnock, one of the co-founders of Adobe. John Warnock's son, Chris Warnock, requested that Slimbach design the typeface as a tribute to his father in 1997. It was later released as a commercial font by Adobe in 2000 under the name Warnock Pro.

MORE FROM BLOOMSBURY POETRY

If you enjoyed *An Interesting Detail*,
you might like *A Method, A Path*
by Rowan Evans:

PLAINSONG

Before: 'fretted with veins of ivy,' now
'fronting the weight of it,' red footprints in
black mud. Looking for a key in the hall.

Children stand between neon candles
of dogwood, guarding some narrative.

And every one that moves. Strips of hill
and cloud become a sheaf, where usually
I describe the machine of language. No,
this time syntax doesn't whirr.